So it is so lovely gifted you Blessing, mine

JOURNEYING

THE

WATERS

Enjoy!

A Book of Poetry and Prose
HUGUETTE M. FOREST-COULTRY

Journeying the Waters
Copyright © 2020 by Huguette M. Forest-Coultry

Tellwell Talent
www.tellwell.ca

ISBN
978-0-2288-0531-1 (Paperback)
978-0-2288-0532-8 (eBook)

"A ship in harbor is safe,
but that is not what it is built for."
John Augustus Shedd
1859 – 1931

"Change, is the only constant in life."
Heraclitus
Greek Philosopher
500 BC

~ PRAISE FOR JOURNEYING THE WATERS ~

Huguette whom I have always known as 'Mike,' so exquisitely tells our stories and reminds us to look, listen and love. And especially to not be afraid! Mike's vision and ability to hear and speak with delicate song yet strong feelings seem to access both her French and English roots. Her close connection to a Higher Power is woven throughout. This book is a "keeper!"

Joan Lawrence; Founder of Joly Arts Works
Arts and Sociology Degrees
Victoria, BC., Canada

By describing connection with art, music, people and nature, this poetry collection reminds us to be present to the moment. Wisdom messages shine throughout these works with Mike's reflection of her soul self. This is an array of writings that add meaning to our lives.

Mary Menduk; Author of, "Not Even the Artist Knows the Words"
Fernie, BC., Canada

Encountering life with joy and hope, Mike's words paint beautiful pictures and powerful images that provide the reader with the opportunity to have their own first-hand experience of their own life's riches. Her soul-searching words spark within us, our own divinity and encourage us to focus on what's important in life. A true treasure! Count me in for the first print-run!

Oz Parsons; Executive Director, Fernie, BC. Canada and District
Arts Council; 2007-2012
Author of, "Dying to be Born, The Complete Journey from Death
to Birth"

Huguette's poems and stories encourage me to look inward and to make positive changes in my own life. Because of this, I am grateful and thankful that this publication will be available to others who will, through these words, discover something personal and inspiring. Let these words bring you closer to our Creator and Spirit God, and to those around you. May you be blessed while on this amazing journey!

Aline Giesbrecht
Government of Canada employee/28 years of service
Winnipeg, Manitoba, Canada

Within these pages you will experience moments of joy and sadness, struggles and triumphs, nature's fury and glory, all within the human existence. An insightful and thought-provoking read.

Nicole Boulanger; Retired X-ray Technologist
Boulanger Farms; Certified Organic Beef and Grain Producers
Grande Clairière, Manitoba, Canada

Aah…the things you know. My friend, you peek into my soul and put into words the feelings I am often afraid to say out loud. Then you have it wash over me with compassion and love, letting it flow away… resolved. A gift of insight and self awareness awaits as you read each of these stories. I cannot wait for more!

Glenna Perkins
Wood Artist; Lovin' Livin' Unlimited
Jaffray, BC., Canada

Huguette is a true and wise word master who in her exquisite poetry offers wisdom and solace to other journeyers. She reminds each of us that each moment, no matter the obstacles, is precious and to be lived to the full. This is a guidebook for life.

Victoria Lenon
Life & Learning Strategist, Modern Mystic
35 Year companion on the journey
Calgary, AB Canada

Mike's writings do not leave you untouched. It is raw in places, at times rendering a touch of sadness, and at other times, much love. I know her as a writer and as a friend of many decades. I would say that JOURNEYING THE WATERS is a Masterpiece! We will all benefit from her gift.

Rachelle Couturier
Artist, Retired Educator
Calgary, Alberta, Canada

~ AN INTRODUCTION ~

Huguette Micheline Forest-Coultry acquired her nickname 'Mike' from a handsome Alberta man working on the pipelines of the Canadian prairies in the early 1970's. No one seemed able to pronounce her French name, so he quickly settled on his own moniker. They married in 1976 and continue to be an excellent team.

They live in the same Fernie, BC community as their children, where they have been blessed with the ultimate joy of "Grand-parenting!"

A lifetime of creative writing began in 1966 while attending Souris Collegiate Institute in Southwest Manitoba. These compositions would likely not have occurred without the invaluable encouragement of her English literature teacher, Mrs. Irene Oberlin.

Mike's *'Spirit Qwest Ministry'* came to life in Okotoks, Alberta, where she, along with her husband and children, lived for 23 years. Her ministry involved Spiritual Direction, Faith Enrichment, Liturgy and Ritual, 12-Step Recovery work, Personal Growth Counseling as well as Guided Retreat Direction.

She and her husband built and managed the *'Hermitage Retreat Cottage'* on their Okotoks acreage for several years where many were welcomed to rest, respite and meditate, while on their busy journeys through life.

Mike invites you to pursue your own growth as you ponder these words of insight.

IF

If this was it
it would be enough.

If today was the last
I would be satisfied.

If the breathing ends
there will have been ample air.

If my body is stilled
this spirit will go on.

If you believe
that all of our yesterdays
were worthwhile.

If you understand
that we gave what we could.

If you remember
more good than bad.

If tears
are mixed with laughter.

If you accept
that time was ours
to the minute.

If you know
that it was all it was meant to be.

Our last words will never be,
"If only…"

WHAT IS JOY?

It is watching the journey of the ladybug
making its way over a broad green leaf
gently swaying in the breeze.

It is the anticipation of the rainbow of colors
to be revealed in a newly tilled garden
sown with love,
under an early morning sky.

It is the blooming of laughter
from deep within one's soul.

It is the effortless song of love
overwhelming the senses with peace
while holding a newborn infant.

It is the sense of deep-felt accomplishment,
when a difficult problem has been resolved
or a complicated question has been answered.

It is the hoots of laughter
the unbridled smile
on the faces of youth
swinging from a tree rope,
plunging into the cooling river-waters below.

It is the embracing of a world
made better,
by an act of giving.

It is the gifting of wisdom
in the sound of silence.

It is the communion offered
to a stranger who seems lost.

It is the rootedness felt
when walking through a carpet of lush grass
or a sandy shore,
where waves lap gently at one's feet.

It is shadow and light,
exposed while journeying
the forest floor,
soothingly protected by nature's canopy.

It is the satisfaction of being,
while leaving the doing for another day.

It is the moment of revelation,
when oneness with creation
is acknowledged and profoundly felt.

It is the sudden realization
that being who I am,
is enough.

It is knowing that profound joy,
can only be manifested from within.

It is my small moments of truth,
quietly revealed
as life's journey is experienced.

It is gift.
It is grace.

It is the desire to be at one
with the world.

For as it is with all things,
granted by the power of the Creator,
joy is at its best…

                              … when it is shared.

RENEWAL

I fly above and look upon it all,
as if assessing another person's life.

It does me good to detach occasionally,
giving this life an unbiased evaluation.

If I stay too close to it, the lines blur.
I may not recognize where
and how I need to change.

And, if I fly too far from it,
I do not allow myself
possession of it.

So, I must seek balance,
not wishing to change too terribly much,
yet, being wise enough to accept change
as a necessary and positive process.

Allowing the wind to carry me,
where the Divine leads me.

Confident that I am exactly
where I am meant to be,
in this moment.

With that, I will enjoy the currents of air,
while I admire the scenery of my life.

BRUSH STROKES

Before an artist begins a particular work,
many fruitful hours are devoted
to the pondering of ideas.

What might it entail?
How will it look, what shape will it take?
What resources will be used
to help define the concept imagined?

Has enough time been set aside
for the research of a chosen subject?
Will information be gathered from myriad places?

The question is then asked,
"What medium will be used?
Will it be oils, acrylics, pen,
pencil, pastels, chisels or saws?"

What trials and tribulations
might this artist suffer,
while creating such a work?

What effort must be expended
to become one
with an evolving masterpiece?

Will interruptions be tolerated
while toiling in an enclosed space,
or among more natural settings?

Step by step, the strokes are refined,
whether it be on canvas, silk,
wood or other complex materials.

More is perfected.
More is accomplished,
as the personality of the oeuvre
reveals itself.

What bountiful confidence
does it take to then relinquish it?
What vulnerable courage does one need
to give it wings?

To risk all, without condition.
Such is the self-sacrifice attached,
to both Art *and* Love.

STOP

Often, I can be consumed
with trying to make my life
and my world perfect.

When that occurs,
my mind easily falls into a trap.

I become anxious.
At times, I become irritated.
Anger can pervade and consume me.
There is no room left for peace.

"Stop," my inner voice says.
"Be still.
Surrender."

"Recognize the Power
who feeds your spirit,
making your life...
                    ...a dance of joy."

WALLED IN

She stares at the putrid green walls
of the ancient, run-down tenement.
The way they look, is how she feels.

It's an empty kind of room in many ways,
her possessions few.
An emptiness exacerbated by his absence,
but full of the secrets she shares,
with plaster and wallpaper.

It's a one-sided affair,
as an echo reverberates

with every harsh and unforgiving word
she throws at them.

Looking in the mirror, she finds proof
of her agonizing loneliness.
The eyes are vacant.
Lines drawn by sadness, not years.

When he was there,
everything seemed to vibrate with life.
Now, wrenching tears flood
a river called 'Emptiness.'

Lying in a curled-up ball,
she wishes too,
that they would wash and cleanse
the utterly deep despair within.

An absolute void permeates her being.
Is this what they call 'Depression?'

"Where is the strength I have felt
I always possessed," she asks?
The moving on and not looking back.

She has never borne
this excruciating burden, this oppressive reality.
This all-encompassing grief,
compelling her to burrow within sheets and throws
desperately in need of a wash.

Is faith in love truly gone with the last of the wine?
Is permanence an illusion in the mortal mind?
But what of steadfast love?

Is undying commitment and devotion a possibility?
Or, has it been like her conversation with the walls
...one-sided?

Can she find the wherewithal
to move from the bed,
lock the door and walk the river?
Wearing anguish as a coat,
with shadows as company.

Maybe out there, she can move
toward a new horizon,
and morning's light.

Maybe there,
she will find answers.

A REMINDER

Events that touch the soul
seem at times to be more than coincidence.
Those momentous occasions
that can lead to cherished relationships
which form the core of our *'Family of origin'*
and *'Family of choice.'*

Yet, my moments of anger, frustration,
judgement and unmet expectations
can tear the fragile fabric of love.

Today a good reminder is to be kinder,
to be gentler and less hurtful
in unconditional ways.

Acquaintances or mere strangers
should not be the first to see
the best that I can be.

Loving others should come secondly
to loving those living under my own roof!

STILLNESS

It is silence in search of new meaning,
the seeking and receiving of answers
to a deeply personal quest.

It is life and motion,
music and prayer,
an appreciation of the world's magnificence.

It is the running commentary of sharing,
of imparting the little things that nurture.

It is the gift of water, sunlight,
a healing touch,
along with the deep conviction
that all life is sacred.

It is the rituals that impact daily life.
Those wonders and possibilities,
that can easily be taken for granted.

It is both the slow
and swift evolution of ideas,
formed and expressed.

It is the power of the moment
and the progression of acquired wisdom.

Most of all, it is the belief that growth
is not defined by a certain point or destination.

Rather, it is the '*indwelling of Spirit*'
that incessantly defines
the very heart of a living being.

Soul Themes,
Illuminating Light and Love,
Nestling Emptiness,
Savoring Spirit.

STILLNESS:
Readying the soul for conversation.

JAZZ

Late into the night I listen,
serenaded by old musical icons.

Wrapped in a quilt
I have had since youth,
I feel you deep within.
Waiting…
Growing…

Descending into a waking dream
I see you.

A child born of old yet born anew
from a mother's womb.
Life's most perfect gift.
A treasure beyond price.

Rising above me an exquisite
female form appears,
arriving on ethereal wings.

She wears a necklace of ancient
sapphire stones.

Her beauty cannot be described
in mere words.

All thought, all action,
all else but her presence
dissipates into the universe.
Serene, beautiful, gracious.
Sheltering all that is sacred.

She rides the waters of time.
Bringing nature and nurture
to fruition.

Drawing you from the womb
I watch as she cradles you at her breast.
Without words she inspires, teaches,
encourages.

Then, in a voice soft as eiderdown
she murmurs her promise to you,

"I am yours forever more.
You alone are my point of migration."

I feel you somersault
in the sanctuary that is your home.

I watch once again as she takes flight.
I sigh and softly whisper,
"Good-bye, thank-you."

As the end of day approaches
I am joyous, sated.
Immensely grateful
for the smallest of miracles.

YOU FEED ME

I take your heart into my hands.
Its caress is like water to a parched landscape.
You smile and it warms the whole of me.

You have turned the key
to an unfamiliar door.

We walk together under starlight.
So much of my youthful blindness
escapes into the ether,
making way for a new maturity.

I detect within me trust restored,

A life-giving sustenance
to replace my agonizing doubts.

Night breaks into day.

With the sun rising above us
we make love.
I feel you capture all that I am
knowing what I need.

A forced distance is necessary these days
but I am graced with a storm of memories.
Ones that bring a smile to my face.

Little heart secrets
belonging only to you and me.

Our winter demandingly descends upon us.
Yet, I feel the cloak of warmth
that no weather can take away.

Such is the heat of our love.
Rekindled with each thought,
turned into fire,
every time you are near.

TEN

How do the days go by so swiftly?
Yet so slowly?

It seems a forever age since we said, "*Adieu!*"
Then at times it seems only days ago.

I often think to call her and ask her a question
that no one else could answer.
Ones I neglected to ask during her time with us.

Did you know and love
your Grand-mères et Grand-pères?

What was, in your view
your greatest achievement?
Your favourite moment in time?
Your biggest regret?
What would you have done differently?

I do not hear her voice.
Still, I often sense
her presence near.

I know she's not gone from my life.
She awaits our reunion with her,
the reunion of us all,
in the Triune's perfect love.

When she thinks of us,
I know her eyes light up.
She smiles her brilliant smile,
followed by a soft sigh of joy.

She longs that we, her children
remain close to one another,
carrying on the traditions
of hearty food, laughter, praise and song.

She gave us much,
maybe not what was craved
or needed at times.

But other things, that in hope,
have made me a better person.

Characteristics that have fashioned
who I am today.

A better spouse, mother,
grandmother, aunt, niece,
cousin and friend.

On this anniversary
I bow my head and give thanks.

KICKIN' IT

Locked up inside my head.
Mute.
Shut down.

Rocking to the buzz
in my veins.

"Help me,"
just becomes a slur of words.
Meant for someone else, right?

'Cause me, man, I ain't got a problem!
No freaking way!

I'm the next big winner.
Scoring a line, drunk on a dime.
But what in God's name did I just do?

"Hey, someone's hurt!
HELP!
He's not breathing!
HELP!"

It all went wrong!
I killed him with love, man.
Just a little bomb.
Just happiness in a vial.

Crap happens.
I'll pay my time, I'll pull back.
Take a little mini retirement.

No loaded, entitled, so-called friends
to judge me.
No self-righteous prig
messing with my choices.

Not such a bad thing
this hole with bars.

Paying the price, hombre.

Free of charge. Can't complain.
It ain't such a bad stretch.

Time has come.
A copper marches me out.
Trudging along from a van
to a downtown slum.

My time to shine.
Till I piss on the sidewalk.
Or puke on the transit.
And irritate, "*The man.*"

Yeah, I know…
more time
in a concrete box.

Geez, it's been so long.
Can't seem to find
my way home.

Later…
like gawd-dam eons later
we arrive.

With a listless wave
I turn and move through
the flap door of this canvas,
paper, plastic castle that is home.

Everybody's gone.
Even my girl.
Alone…
again.

Everything's cool, right?
Relaxin'
Rockin' back and forth
to some old junky tune.

No worries, man…
not today.
No raging at everything and anything.

Till the excruciating wounds open
and seep from my pores.

Again.
Crushing me.

Agonizing secrets
hidden and seductive,
dragging me back, back...

The only escape being the next trick,
the next drink, the next time I mule.
My next, "Bad!"

Yeah...
next time.

Man, I can't do this!
Just give me something.
Anything...
to take this pain away.

I got no backbone left
against the terror,
the nightmares!

"Come on dude!
Will you take credit,
take me on my word
just one more time?

I promise,
I'll make good, p-l-e-a-s-e?"

A gun is pulled.

BANG!

I guess this time,
the answer is "*No*!"

FALLING

With hibiscus and jasmine
perfuming the tropical air,
I sit swallowing liquid gold.

Wearing purple and orange.
(Who really cares?)

I fall, fall, fall…
into a place so quiet
I can hardly hear myself breathe
nor hear the surrounding sounds
of evening-call.

What is it about sun and surf that heals?
How it profoundly calms the soul.

The Creator whispers
that the love manifested
from the heavens
numbers greater than the stars.

A love even grander
than every grain of sand
counted in this universe!

Covenant and love's promise
set in the beauty of every rainbow,
in the magic of every sunrise and sunset,

letting me know that
what I have
is much more than enough.

Much more than I ever dreamed.
More than I have ever imagined.

To be loved, to be healed,
to be forgiven.

To be ever grateful for eyes that see,
ears that hear nature's murmurings
as well as the voice of others.

But most importantly,
the voice within.

Appreciative of hands and feet
that move where I am led
encouraging me to trust
to be all I am meant to be.

Immersed in desert air
the sense of comfort and peace
is like no other.

So spectacular
it cannot be wholly described
in human language.

Life, at times,
is measured on a scale.
One to Ten...

Ten cannot begin to honor
this astonishing winter paradise.

A verdant green palette,
unknown in prior, more youthful years.

It is only with age
and accompanying wisdom
that one can fully appreciate this offering
of peace, serenity and tranquility.

As opportunities arise
I will endeavor to pay it forward.

Yet I doubt there will ever be sufficient time,
to repay all the goodness and abundance
endowed me in this wondrous life.

But living in gratitude
is a good start!

IMPACT

Chatting with co-workers
who were dear buddies
the world seemed to be inviting and kind.
He cherished his friendships
and the place he called home.

He was a lineman, a job he loved.
A guy who took risks every day
making sure that he or others,
were never injurcd or killed

due to an oversight
or a lapse in concentration.

He had often said how powerful the surge of current was
when he held a bundle of cable in his hands.
He respected the danger that could be wrought.
How death was only ever a live wire away.

He was coming home to a pecan pie.
For him, the knowledge that this delicacy awaited
put a grin on his face.
No one could bake that pie like Momma did!

It was in the sharing with family and friends,
where he could relax and truly feel grounded.

He rounded the long, sharp curve,
one he had driven too many times to count,
knowing the road, trusting his ability.

But on this day, he overshot the curve.
In the space of milli-seconds
all was perpetually changed.

For him, and the ones left behind.
His friends survived.
He was my hero,
investing time with me while he was home.

I was the sometime daughter his parents never had.
I delighted in crushing pecans and rolling pie crusts,
lovingly taught by his mother.

A Mom he incessantly teased, hugged,
and gave a big smack of a kiss to,
while she giggled like a schoolgirl!

Today, there are no more kisses,
no more of his deep laughter,
no more carousing to Beatles' tunes,
while singing off-key.

All I have left is a solitary rose
to place on an oak coffin,
while rivers of tears
stream down my stricken face.

These many years later,
the most precious of memories
has us washing his beloved sports coupe.

He with the sponge, me with a chamois.
The 'Bon Ami Powdered Cleanser' in hand
making sure the wheel rims sparkled.

That was my job, as it was his least favorite.
I found it an easy, enjoyable task
beneath the sun's ochre hue.

Occasionally, a battle ensued,
the hose becoming the weapon of choice
in our lop-sided war.

The loser; relegated to using a mere bucket.
An unfair proposition each and every time!
To this day I revel in the fact of winning
our very last scrimmage.

He blessed me with an uncomplicated
yet deep-rooted friendship.
One very few people knew existed.

He was there for me
while I struggled with my emerging,
late adolescent identity.

He generously allowed me his time, his wisdom.
For that I will be eternally grateful.

I have yet to roll a pie crust since his passing.
Pecans will always and forever
bring his face and laughter to mind.

But now when remembering,
I can finally smile…
without the tears.

THE SHARING OF QUERIES

What echoes within us when catastrophe strikes?
When the words, "It could have been any one of us!"
resound.

What words form and appear in the mind's dialogue,
after loss and tragedy?

Is it time to truly engage in life
in the here and now,
and not simply go through the motions?

What about a family excursion?
Reveling in the beauty of an environment
that may not recently have been noticed
or appreciated.

If not with family, then friends,
the ones who so often hear, "Soon, truly."
"We need to get together soon!"

Or, maybe it is time
to relish the world in solitude,
while birds chirp their blessings.

Where can more minutes and hours be found
to share with ones who are loved and cherished?

Does scheduling more fun,
amusement and wonderment come naturally?

What gratitude is expressed
when there is an unexpected,
serendipitous, kind of day?

It is never too late for new beginnings,
whether physical, emotional, or spiritual.

Victims of sudden death,
have no more time on this planet.
Tragedies causing death
often lead to an altered sense
of what is important and what is trivial.

The present may be the perfect day
for new choices,
options that lead to more intimacy,
more sharing, of daily life's ups and downs.

While standing assured
that all life has purpose
and that it may be time to revisit old values.

To approach innovative ideas with courage
means a personal choice.

When pertinent questions need profound answers,
it may be time to listen
and to respond.

OCTOBER

By candlelight the wind woos me.
The sound of geese scurrying across the lake
soaks into my bones and brings peace.

Squirrel and chipmunk
quiet their daily pursuit of food
and malleable resources
to line their winter nests.

Robin, solitaire, nuthatch and flicker
have gone to bed
after an intrepid bath,
bringing awareness of placement
in their pecking order.

Cloud and purple sky mix
to close the day,
bringing instant darkness
to the landscape.

But, not to my soul.
It is light and bright
with the recompense of faith.

A last night to appreciate
what creation has brought to my door.

Autumn's amplified gifts noted,
as another lake season comes to a close.

There are few words to express
this degree of gratitude.
No prayer to suffice.

After a quiet night's rest
my heart will once again welcome
tomorrow's bounteous gifts.

GRACE

Grace to be.
Grace to have.
Grace to hold.

Gifts of sight,
of hearing,
of love.

Grace and gifts breathed upon the air,
dispersed upon the wind.
Grace scattered upon the waters.

Grace within,
received and given.

Spirit intact,
profoundly fulfilled
by gift and grace.

THE BECKONING OF WINTER

Wafting smells of leavened wheat
harvested from clearings of tilled ground.

Fish pulled from shallow, rippling streams
or the depths of aqua lake water.

Wondrous forests expanding
as multitudes of seed hover on the wind.
Falling,
to softly nest.

Forked lightening, roaring thunder,
billowing cloud, invite drenching rain
to nurture scorched lands.

Row upon row of pendulous grapes
await to be turned from fruit to wine.

Too soon for many,
gloomy, dark clouds gather and swirl.

The wind suddenly howls
breathing snowflakes into the air.

T'is the season in this northern clime,
when gifts are manifested.

A nickel found when one has none.
A listening ear among thousands closed.
A precious embrace conquering abject fear.

Shelter offered, nothing asked in return.
Pearls of wisdom dispelled
soothing an aching heart.

Through the ages ancient civilizations
have been brought to life,
then died as all things must.

Till an Eastern star, brighter than millions
hung upon a silent night
broken by angels' song.

A child is born.

The perfect model of love,
forgiveness and compassion,
who taught us well, the gift of miracles.

LOST

He no longer pays attention
to the darkness of night.
Nor for that matter, the bright light of day.

No longer caring,
he lives in a blinded state of apathy.

How did he get here?
When did he lose touch?

When did life become so overwhelming?
Losing all confidence.
Losing all.

He cannot remember the last time
he gazed at the constellations
or watched nightfall or the moon's rise.
Has it been weeks… or months?

At one time even a solitary, glimmering star
seemed enough to help find relevant answers.

Lately he hasn't even taken notice of the sun.
Keeping the aging burgundy velvet drapes closed tightly,
against an outside world he no longer comprehends.

Looking now through the bevelled glass
with its ugly paint-chipped casing,
he wonders if it is warming the world
or manifesting winter's brittle cold?

And how had he not noticed
the declining condition of his own house?
An ideal home, set in an ideal neighbourhood,
so proudly acquired decades ago.

Seasons mean little while trapped
in wretched despondency.

No longer hungry,
no longer concerned about what to wear.
No longer maintaining any regimen of self-care.

No longer interested… in anything.
A mere shell with no purpose.

Sand rattles through his core,
quenched and quieted by a flask of magic elixir
poured into a Baccarat crystal cocktail glass.

Proof of what life used to be
before she so unceremoniously walked away.

Before an excellent job turned into a pink slip
releasing him from the only work he had ever known,
rendering him a no longer needed commodity of yester-year.

A liability.
Not an asset.

There is no helping hand.
No room for one iota of mercy.
They have the gall to call it progress!

The golden notes of whiskey
quell the pain, the anxieties, the fear.
Drowning out the ever-present insomnia,
the night terrors.

There is one thing he knows and knows intimately:
an earthly paradise once sought
is no longer within grasp.

Hell has grabbed him by the throat!

Nothing much matters anymore.
There is no longer room in this ravaged heart
to want change, to seek it, to devour it,
to be who he once was.

No, the shell is truly empty.
There is no strength to carry on.
No reserve to count on.
No meaning to the length or breadth of days.

"O God, if there truly is a room prepared for me,"
he whispers pleadingly.

"Take me. I am ready.
If not, rouse me from this desolation,
stir me to action.
Provoke this lost and tortured soul to know
that transformation is a possibility."

Even now... even for me!"

ROCK CANDY

Layered chunks
Shifting shapes

Glittering crystals
Smoky grays
White-faced moons

Sedona reds
Speckled eggs
Licorice stacks

Pearled agates
Zebra stripes
Golden ambers
Sculpted hearts
Ancient stone

Tumbling song
upon the shoreline.

Rock candy
mingled with lake tears
because
you are not here.

A HYMN OF GRATITUDE

Fertile is my being.
Full of love, full of blessing.

Every season around me
and within me
is nurtured.

My fullness is leavened
with salt of this earth.
Not too much nor too little.

My roots are firmly planted.
My seeded being reaps
the bounty of harvest.

Though I may thirst,
providence provides.

So that I may never be too thirsty
nor too empty.

My heart thrums with life and love
fulfilled beyond all telling.

Though at times I am needy, unsure.

Consequently,
I must turn toward the Light.

I will lift my arms in praise, in petition.
Blessed to live in grateful thanksgiving.

FIRE

Billowing clouds turn the world to grey.
These are not thunderclouds.
They are fire clouds tinged with red,
creating colored silhouettes of this mountain vista.

It is raining embers and ash
turning the tipi to polka-a-dot displays
looking like snowfall,
turned black in mid-August.

Across the lake,
an inferno consumes all in its path.

Blessedly, there is no tragedy
or loss of life on this waterfront.
Much of nature seems to take little notice
of this dismal disaster.

Osprey fervently dive for their breakfast.
Eagles skim the water
possibly seeking fresher air
and a good catch, in this summer's
abominations of nature.

Salmon, unaware of predators
jump and stir the water into ever-widening circles.

Geese practice formations, readying for journey.
The young struggle to apply instinctive behavior.
The V's presently look more like wide U's.

Grasshoppers have not yet overtaken this landscape.
Other areas have been devastated by their infestation.

Here, butterfly and beetle, squirrel and chipmunk,
keep up their happy travel
in an ever-constant quest for nectar and food sources.

Nuthatch and junco tuck their wings and gather speed,
rushing, each attempting to be first at the birdbath.
A unique one, conjured upon a gnarled stump
rescued from last year's spring run-off.

Chickadees join in avian play.
Water droplets fly,
while they bat their wings in cool relief,
standing on pretty stones
displayed in water-filled crockery.

Throughout the day,
loons scatter on the lake's surface
oblivious to the sound of motors,
compelling water to tumble and tremble.

Swallows bury themselves
in their cool sandy nests,
dotting the cliffs of the shoreline.
Later, they will dive for their supper,
then retreat.

Bats will make a late evening appearance
snagging bugs from the air and the water's surface.

The sun, a giant ball of red
colors the waves a shimmering copper.
It will swiftly drop from the sky
as smoke clouds reflect its unrivaled glory.

No moon, however full,
can possibly penetrate this canopy.
No stars will gleam in this night sky.

Another day has ended.
Time for rest, so that tomorrow
we may watch again,
hungry for weather's change.

Before sleep overcomes me,
I voice a sincere prayer for those less fortunate,
those many thousands who have been ravaged
by these furious flames.

Also, one for those who risk all
in an ever-widening battle
against roaring, persistent fires.

And yet another is uttered toward the heavens
for a change to clouds that loom above,
showering respite upon man, beast and nature.

With gratitude for all that is well
and acceptance of all that is less than perfect,
I close my eyes and dream of soft rain.

IS THIS LIVING?

Constrained by the gloom
of night's silence, despair thrives
in that room they call a mind.

Thrashing emotions bursting to emerge,
only to be harbored within a broken heart.

Examinations and surgical proof cannot be denied.
Cruelties of the past can no longer be hidden.
A body suddenly stripped of the illusion of normalcy.

No one listens.
No one who gives a damn!
The medicine men verbalize
in complicated medical lingo.
No inclusiveness exists.

The morning sky is filled
with crystalline flakes
falling from the heavens.
A December day pronouncing its arrival.

The outside world is perversely unattainable
to someone confined to a crowded space,
perpetually filled with the putrid smells
of medicine, bleach and the foul
bottled sentiments of desolation and loss.

Drowning in visceral pain,
spontaneous, burning tears are shed alone.
The cries of a confused and muddled mind.

Time no longer measured in days,
but months.

Once again, a casualty, a prisoner,
attached to various gadgets
promising life to ravaged tissues.
Craving escape changes nothing.

Hearty laughter erupts in a hallway.
This weary being cannot remember
an uninhibited laugh or a moment of joy,
while buried among ratty institutional linens.

Courage seems just a word with little meaning.
The prospect of hope seems an unlikely dream.

Where is my knight in shining armor,
the one who will promise miracles?

Maybe tomorrow, he will pull up on his mighty steed,
and lead this broken being to a source of new life.

Riding briskly, vigorously, to a safe enclave,
a place of protection, a haven for healing.

SURRENDER

I wanted to listen to music coming from the laptop,
yet was drawn instead to follow the music of the heart.

I fancied a walk in the brisk, jostling, autumn wind
but a quiet voice spoke, "Retreat to the tranquil quiet of
the fire.

Watch as it burns down to coals, warming the night.
Rest while the hum of the ancient Frigidaire
sings its own, three-note song."

I take some time to journal
and an inner voice speaks once more.
"Today, write words of encouragement
for others."

I yearned to watch the stars
and last night provided the gift of the universe
blinking at this world's fingertips.

I intended to burrow into a novella
but instead, the air divulged the gift of a psalm.

I wanted wisdom for the journey.
The invitation given was to live in the moment.
That wise insight would be revealed
in time.

I was seeking courage to be more vulnerable,
more assured in relationships.
Clarity was again gently exposed
and trust regained
even while in the throes of uncertainty.

I craved the power of Light.
Darkness was unmasked,
disclosing the difference
between truth and falsehoods.

Guided always
from impoverishment to inner riches.

My days lack for nothing.

T'IS THE SEASON

The stars shine bright,
as translucent mist hangs
in the bitter, fortifying air.

While walking the river's edge
breath's vapor tells the story
of the season's inescapable wintry weather.

As the cold bites through me
I approach the cottage.
Through the glass of the sliding door
I see the radiant embers of a fire I banked hours ago.

I move toward the fieldstone hearth
through shimmering light,
reds and oranges shadowing the pine walls.

There is no need to illuminate the room.
The vintage Tiffany lamp needs not be lit
while I make my way to a favorite chair.

It is no hardship for me to fall gladly
into the well-worn recliner,
and wrap chilled shoulders
in a red and black Scottish-plaid throw.

I am grateful for all that life provides
as I quietly listen to carols
that bring a smile to so many millions
on this festive eve.

I sense in a profound way the blessings of the day
and the yesterdays of a year one week away
from becoming a memory.

The comfort and joy of family and faithful friends
will encircle one and all come morning.
Voices will rise in joy while laughter abounds.
Gifts will be hurriedly opened to cheers
and grateful thanks.

The kitchen will divulge its treasures
of food and drink, devotedly prepared.

The aroma of cranberry tea and mulled wine
imbued with cinnamon and cloves
will leave scintillating scents
floating through the air.

The turkey and ham's splendid roasting aromas
will waft from room to room.

All that is true, all that is valued,
all that is needed, all that is wanted,
will be treasured,
while surrounded by nurture
and precious love.

YOU ~ MY STRENGTH

There is a tempest of thought and emotion
that you have always calmed,
quelled and made positive.

Your acceptance, your acknowledgement
of who I am has never waivered.

Your vision, your truth, touches me
at the most opportune times.

You are you, and I am me.
But together, we are a force of one!

AUGUST NIGHT

Blue ridged mountains
absorb light and sound.
Laughter fills the air.

Music thumps against pine and cedar.
Whoops erupt
as percussion rhythms
weave through the air.

Cheering voices resound.
All are ecstatic.

This summer night reveals stars
amidst lazy cloud formations.
Equally comforting to lake life
and humankind.

Friends, old and new
share this annual ritual.

No rain on this August night.
Fires forbidden
during this hazardous summer season.

The horizon glows gold.
Candles flicker in safe,
eclectic vessels.

Subdued light shadows bird bath
and seed feeder alike.

Dawn will bring renewed joy
to winged creatures.
Delight fills the heart while watching them
fully engaged in their flight and play.

Soon, night will drift
into early morning hours.

With spirit rekindled
nothing more is needed.

Nothing more is necessary.

EARLY MAY MEMORIES

Long narrow fingers crossed
on the belly of his small frame.
He'd grown a modest paunch,
invisible really,
unless he purposely extended his middle,
as he occasionally did
with a mix of pride and humor.

Broad forehead, sharp cheekbones.
A nose that could not deny his ancestry.

A book by his side, often Louis L'Amour.

Ignoring his previously held ideology
of the so-called, sloppy 60's hippie era,
he grew his thick, pin-straight hair

over his ears in the late 1970's
amusing every one of his six children.

Resplendent in a suit and tie.
Posture always perfect.
Shoes polished to a gleam.

Brogues, replaced by sneakers
as consequences of a stroke took its toll.

A bay-colored sweater
with suede accents and patches.
My all-time favorite.

A wide smile, gap-toothed in places.
A choice he made letting nature take its course.
Close mouthed, a tick at the jaw line
warned of tension.

Nearly black, penetrating eyes
twinkled as he laughed.
His brilliant tenor voice rose and carried.

Gold-dust notes hovering upon the air,
especially in song, which was his passion.

Intelligence and wit obvious.
Learning; a life-long infatuation.

He loved a good joke, an easy read, nature.
He cherished profoundly the gifts of faith
and the promise of hope.

A man to be remembered;
handsome, steadfast, faithful.

Many hearts miss his presence.

AN UNKNOWN

Rising from the waters from whence you came
you are cradled by rolling rock.

A slight breeze wraps itself around
this sun-dappled, late-May morning.

Who are you, what is your story?
What was your purpose?

You once had a voice.
Was it soft and lilting
or was it rough and gravel-toned?

Were your last words of love?
Or anguish?

Were they possibly words of anger
or even rage?

Where were you headed?
Was it your destiny to lie, life expired,
upon the waters of a lakeshore
close to the foot of a rugged wooden cross?

You once had hands that were useful to you.
Did they lovingly knead,
or have a carpenter's knack?

Did they cradle a nursing child,
or entertain an artist's touch?

Did they reel a line or carve?
Or chop wood for winter's warmth?

Were your features young
or traced with age?
What were your dreams?

Was water such a friend
that it claimed you for its depths,
embracing you in finality?

Or was water a place where you
could hide or be hidden,
hopefully to never be found?
Nor to be seen again?

For how long was this lake your grave?
Was it weeks, months or seasons?

Did you move with the currents of spring,
making your way to our doorstep
of bleached wood stairs?
Feet still in slippers, canvas coat,
what clues do they give us?

Were you in a rush?
Were you pursued or forced
to this watery end?

Or, were you simply comfortable,
unassuming of a disaster that would befall you?

There are many questions and few answers.
Within me an innate desire yearns
to impart your spirit with this certain knowledge.

Many have been impacted by your presence here.
We too feel a sad sense of loss.

We are also grateful that someone
may now come forward to claim you,
saying, "Yes, we have a name.
We will honor a life lived.
We will honor its end."

FROM BLINDNESS TO SIGHT

Such troubling compulsions...
to be right
to be in control,
to control
to cling to what is known
to succeed
to be perfect
when perfection is not attainable.

Easily drawn into...
inferiority, mistrust
procrastination, isolation
disapproval and despair.

Which often leads to...
extreme vigilance, anxiety
manipulation and avoidance.

Involving...
the fear of moving forward
or the dread of looking back.

Fears of...
intimacy
abandonment
vulnerability
commitment
conflict and poverty.

Most often resulting in careless choices,
inappropriate decisions
and inexplicable sorrow.

Yet a deep inner voice softly calls out,
waiting, wanting to be heard.

"Be not afraid, trust your own journey.
Believe your own story.
Do the work as needed when needed.

Embrace risk.
Share without condition.
Love without condition.

Replace negatives with positives
knowing there is no timeline.

Believe in healing.
Believe in self-worth,
in forgiveness,
and in the forgiveness of others.

Release the past.

Trust in Divine wisdom.
Trust in the Divine.

Let go of doubt.

Express truth.
Believe in prayer.
Begin with, "Thank-you."

Resolve one little thing now.
Believe that progress and success
begin with one little thing.

It is the profound first step
to rewarding achievement
and monumental healing.

Be tenacious.

Challenge your deepest self
to be all you can be,
without shame, without blame.

Pass on the gifts received.

And know...
. . . that you are loved."

THE GLORY DAYS OF JUNE

Sunshine and a soft breeze permeate the skin.
Cliff swallows and dragon flies, juncos and nuthatch,
June bugs and butterflies embrace the wind.
Bald eagles soar through the lofty draft.

The northern flicker's beating-beak rhythm
fills the air.
Creek rapids tumble over limestone
while fish jump and osprey dive.

Fishing boats chug in the early morning hours.
Cattails and grasses sway,
squirrels sail gracefully
from tree to tree.

Solitude and serenity encompass all.
Nothing more to fill the day
but to walk in gratitude.

I HAVE NO NAME

I lay in a grave, a tomb of rubble
with many thousands.

We are here,
shoulders against legs,
legs against heads,
arms against feet,
thrown together by catastrophe.

I know not who lays beside me,
woman, child or man.
People who once were family.

People, so very many
who may have never known one another.
We sleep now,
a bloated, unrecognizable
mass of death.

My own will never know
where these bones of mine rest.

No marker to show who I am.
No date recalling my birth.
Only one will remain
in the consciousness of humankind.

Tuesday, January 12, 2010.

A stark reminder of rumbling earth,
while imperceivably
towering walls of ocean water strike
with little advance warning.

Like all of us
in this Haitian hole,
today...
     ... I have no name.

DEAREST CHILD

There is a life you are about to begin.
A life you know nothing about.

You do not yet realize how long we have waited
for it to truly begin,
outside of the womb's protection.

You are one of the fortunate children of the world.
You have parents who want you so very much.
Two people who love and are in love,
a love you may someday experience,
but do not fathom now.

You will arrive already cherished
by so many people.
It matters not that you do not know us yet.
We are here for you,
"No matter what!"
No matter when or how.

You will have sibling love to welcome you
and protect your smallness
and to help you grow
through learned and shared experience.

The life you will have
may be short or long,
lent to this world by the Creator.
May it be filled with goodness and grace.

Cherish each day you are given.
You will be born into prosperity,
born free in a democratic society,
free to choose how you will live out your days.

Not threatened by war or famine,
by persecution or dictatorship.
Never take it for granted.

There will be challenges.
Birth itself will be one of your greatest.

We will be there to welcome you
into a sometimes cold, harsh world.
We will protect you when we can
then watch you take wing.

We will applaud your arrival, little one.
May your every moment
culminate in wisdom.

Even when struggles
for peace and right living
imbue your world.

Blessings upon you.
Welcome into the family of humanity.
You have one life to live.
Live it well.

May you always be satisfied
that you have given it your best.

WITNESSING TO LOVE

When witnessing to love
we must plow through
the muddiness of intimacy.

How easy it is at times for the you and me
to become 'we.'
At other times it creates hurdles
that seem nearly impossible to overcome.

Where is the balance allowing our personalities,
strengths, weaknesses and perspectives
to be honored?

Where is the equality in attaining the flow
that goes with give and take?

Where is the capacity to accept and demonstrate
without doubt, sincere expressions of love?
Even while finding it difficult to convey self-love.

It is in the ultimate union of trust,
commitment and companionship
that couples make their own way to one-ness.
To that delicate place where both feel less needy,
in tune with each other's dreams and desires
leading to passion in all things.

There is a voice given to each of us,
one we must learn to recognize.

The voice of love that puts thoughts to words,
giving bodies, minds and hearts the gift to freely share,
especially when things are particularly difficult.

It is not meant that we always guess
at the fragile state of the other.
We need to know it.
And that is only possible
in the spoken sharing.

So, let us trust our inner voices,
our fragile hearts with one another
and fully know this vow of love
is strong, true and enduring.

No matter the currents that at times
seem to divert us from our true purpose.

That goal of unity
where you can be you
and I can be me.

Recognizing that together,
we form the strongest whole.
Better by the fact that we stand together
and not alone.

DESERT PLACES

Silence
Solitude
Retreat
A dwelling forged from the sands of time.

A hallowed offering
A time to detach
To disengage
Separated from commitment and expectation.

Mystery
Light
Grace
Descending
Like the soft patter of rain.

Past
Present
Future
Melding into one serene moment.

Calm
Content
Yet somewhat shaken
while the gift of revelation
makes itself known.

This is an *interior desert*, housing wisdom.
A sacred place, through which the Divine
can be experienced in myriad ways.

Where deep and true meaning is conveyed.
Where direction is often divulged.

The distance from here to there,
is only ever...

    ...a prayer away.

STONE TO STONE

Walking vigilantly,
often slipping from stones
that lead to the other side.

Moving guardedly
to the opposite shore
of judgment, pain, fear,
of a corroding, invasive numbness.

There is no map through the angst
of suspicion,
of broken relationships.
The pervasive
stabbed-heart feeling
of betrayal.

A crippling quagmire of despair
blinds the way to the next foothold.

If tethered to resentment and anger
the bitter heart withers.

Laughter fades
and becomes a distant memory.
Dreams perish for lack of hope.

So once the wretched tears are spent,
after multiple slips and falls,
settle upon the bloom of a new and verdant shore.

Then listen.
Wisdom awaits.

Upon the wind a troubadour optimistically cries out,
"Push through, you are not drowning.
Be the fierceness, the power and strength needed
to reclaim life, trust, love and intimacy."

And on this day, I will.

EMOTION…

…immobilizes body and soul
when imprisoned by anxiety.

Ants seem to be scurrying
through matter and bloodstream
building hills of fear and inertia.

A creeping lethargy paralyzes the brain
of anything but menacing memories
allowing ancient slow-motion videos
to run on an endless loop.

How close is the grasp of insanity?
How long can one play a fictitious role
in the grand theatre of daily life?
Days, weeks, months, possibly years?

How easy it is to under-appreciate one's mental,
emotional and spiritual balance and well-being.
An equilibrium hard fought to attain.

Is the inner work never done?

For triggers still exist.
The reaction is immediate
overwhelming the senses
at the most inopportune times.

The tricks the human mind can perform,
do not put the rabbit back in the hat.

So...what to do?

BREATHE
PRAY
FORGIVE
LOVE
and BELIEVE
in the eventual
ultimate and permanent power
of authentic healing.

SHAPES

How does vocabulary
shape all human life?

What is it within,
that dictates emotion and truth?
Why must it be so difficult at times?

That movement from a negative trait
to a new one that breathes life and joy.

There may not be a firm answer
while meditating today.

Acknowledging and naming the words
that impact each of us
is a sound launching point.

Along with the belief that the very best
within us is achievable.

Allowing life's journey of learning to continue.

From:
Denial to Acceptance
Brokenness to Healing
Self-Rejection to Self-Appreciation

From:
Weakness to Strength
Intention to Action
Pain to Joy
Doubt to Trust
Finding Fault to Forgiveness

From:
Anxiety to Peace
Judgement to Compassion
Resistance to Release
Lack of Knowledge to Wisdom
Isolation to Connection
Dis-Ease to Ease
False Expectations to Reality

From:
Victim to Survivor
Surviving to Thriving

Estrangement to Intimacy
Self-Neglect to Self-care
Fear to Bravery

Taking each optimistic, affirming word
and making it an integral part
of a personal lexis.

Moving away from the negative.
Embracing possibility,
hope and love.

LIMITLESS GRATITUDE

Nature's majestic display surrounds me.
Geese gather into fall formations.
Loons hurl their call over the waters.

Droplets of diamonds
dimple varying surfaces of water.

I cannot run.
Therefore, I beg the young spotted doe
to prance about for me.

I cannot swim.
Therefore, I ask the schools of fish
to be water gymnasts,
so that I may laugh at their antics.

Currently, jetting through clouds
is not an option.

While wrapped in a colorfully striped hammock
on this cloudless afternoon,
I close my eyes and dream of soaring
with a family of eagles
who have made their home in a dying pine,
one bay away from our camp.

I cannot fish.
But as I watch, an osprey plunges into deep waters.
Struggling to keep a grasp, he flies above me.
Preening, he shows me his Kokanee catch.

Moving quickly
is presently an impossibility.
Yet, it does not yield sorrow.

I smile, as the chattering chipmunks
run to me proudly.
Showing off their precious finds
for hidden winter morsels.

I watch in great awe the Momma squirrel,
willing to let me be her audience as the soil flies.
A midden is being constructed
for the cold winter season ahead.

I may be limited by this earthly form called body.
Nonetheless, I can sing for joy with eyes that see.

I can laugh at nature's power to amuse.
I can and will manifest gratitude
for being graced with a summer home
on a cliff by water's edge.

On this sun swept day
I will quiet my soul
and absorb into my spirit
all the universal gifts
so abundantly given me.

THE DREAM

I'll read you a dream, she said
while gliding back and forth
in her favourite chair.

The young girl's eyes open wide,
brows raised in question.
Smiling, she keeps silent…
waiting, anticipating.

Would you like that?

She nods, slithering to the floor,
looking up beyond the woman's ankles
and knees, beyond the heft of her chest
into chocolate eyes,
deeply inset and gilded
with flecks of green.

The dream I read
brings you untold treasure.
A gift that ought never to be wasted.

It is layered in many assorted colours,
in many different shapes.

The dream is wrapped in gossamer feathers.
Sparkling like enchanting wings
bedecked in threads of diamonds.

The dream brings a blossoming of feelings
at times both light and burdensome
spaced only by a millisecond,
recorded in the gong
of the ancient parlour clock.

It bears the ultimate of joys,
but also the agony of painful sorrows.

The dream I read
has no beginning and no end,
not unlike a gleaming band
wrought in gold.

It is ultimately simple yet frequently
intricate and complicated.

Do you want to know
what the dream is called?

Oh yes, Mimi, please!

Well, my precious Rose
the dream is called,
"*LOVE.*"

A MORNING OFFERING

O perfect morning, Creator's great gift.
The beauty of a sun rising and coloring my world,
dappling hues of yellow upon hibiscus,
tangerine, lemon and mango trees.

The sounds of a waking world
that too often ignores the great works
of Mother Earth and Father Sky.
Not mindful enough of gratitude
for what is freely and compassionately given.

Perfect gifts that I will be conscious of this day,
as you welcome and include me
in this conversation of love.

BREAKING SILENCE

Restless souls hunker under bridges
or upon park benches.
Heavenly peace… only a dream.

Calm… a foreign word
where children live in fear
of their own kin
or oppressive bullies.

No serenity amongst the violence
in too many homes and hearts.

Nothing holy about war
raging upon desert sands
and rugged mountain terrain.

Brilliance and clarity blighted
by rampant consumerism
while people go unfed,
unsheltered.

No tenderness or caring
in the experience of rejection
as young women still give birth
in filthy public bathrooms and dark back alleys.

Who are the shepherds
who will recognize the hurt
in each of these faces?

Will you and I find the courage
to drum loudly the reality of pain
so prevalent before us?

Will we bring gifts to the table
of communication and compassion
into our homes and into our world?

Will we bring a divine moment
to a people steeped in loneliness,
hunger and fear?

Will we bring the star
to shine in tortured lives?

Or will we knowingly live in the dark
momentarily sated with food,
drink and rowdy gatherings?

It is time to replace alienation with love,
and scatter it upon the earth.

All the while pondering
and remembering
the most precious gift of all.

The gift of Blessed Peace
showered upon this hallowed night.

CONFUSED

A question is asked.
It is instantly misinterpreted.
Just can't seem to get it right!

Does she truly desire a sincere
and genuine answer?

Stonewalling
seems to have become the norm.

What does it take to listen, to hear,
to respond and be receptive to change?

What does it take to reply
without judgement
and accept without hurt?

Whatever it is,
it is not being revealed tonight
while burning the midnight oil.

Maybe tomorrow
things will become clearer.
So that our conversation can continue
in a kinder way.

So that truth, vision and dreams
can be honestly shared.

For the possibility
that things are irreparable
is simply not acceptable.

With courage let us both refuse
to give up hope.

Let's hold on to the dream
and desire only the best
of what makes us… us.

WALLOWING BENEATH THE PALMS

Shadowed from the incessant heat of the sun
while branches sway,
sweetly caressed by a soft, scented breeze.

Bougainvillea flowers in coral, reds and pinks,
cavort through the windy air.

Let the day unfold.
No thought of lists,
commitments or schedules.

Nothing to interfere with the gift of lethargy
bestowed upon this wondrous, sun-filled day.

Breakers collide with the shoreline
composing nature's concerto.

An ocean calls, while tumbling shells
reach water's edge.

The mass of varying shapes and sizes
reveal a gift.
Sea-glass twinkles and questions arise.

What form did this originally take?
Who brought this aged piece to fruition?
Was it purchased?

Or, was it in the possession
of the craftsman who lovingly molded it
above the coal's once raging inferno?

Why is it indigo-colored rather than the sea green
that is more prevalent here?

Thousands, maybe millions of fragments
lay beneath the sands of time
travelling from afar,
tumbling through vast waters
in an oceanic tango.

What was its original purpose?
How many miles has it travelled,
through expansive roiling waters?

Every piece with its own history.
A familiar story,
one that can be equated to life's journey.

Unique and beloved.

BREATH OF THE SPIRIT ~ 2000

We can shine bright,
nourished, revived, warmed
by a universal Presence.

No need to hide.
No need for shame.

The only need ~
Letting go!

Opening self to new and fresh yearnings.
Carving space and time
for innovative dreams and possibilities.

Clouds will occasionally materialize
chasing the warming rays of the sun.
Yet, they do rapidly disperse.

The breath of Spirit,
once again nudging them away.

Cleansing, renewing, refreshing the soul.
Showering all with grace.
Pouring forth goodness.

Letting life awaken to all that can be.
Making way for more,
much more.

In the gentle light of discovery
a powerful truth is exposed.
The manifestation of Spirit,
has always existed.

Breathing into my dark corners
through all time and circumstance,
coaxing me, inviting me and welcoming me
into this new and dazzling millennial journey.

SEW WELL

Stitch by stitch

It may come to life from scraps
gratefully found in an antique trunk,
tucked into the corner of an ancient attic
many long years ago.

One passed down from a generation
nearly forgotten.
Its perusal not undertaken until now.

A container overflowing
with someone else's memories,
ones they could not give up.

A nice long strip of Mother's wedding gown
hidden in folds of seasonal clothing
at the back of a closet,
will fashion a delicate border.

While wandering and sight-seeing
through a quaint village
the eye catches a small, attractive shop.
Where the perfect pattern
long sought, is finally found.

There are pieces traded, even bolts,
that are no longer to one's taste
or the stitching, for one reason
or another has stopped.

Whether it be age, or illness,
or even the taking-up of a new craft
that turns the page onto a blank palette.

Stitch by stitch

They work bent over a sewing machine
or standing side by side, needle in hand
around a large wooden frame
over which the material
is stretched and secured.

At times they are solitary
and occupied with their own singular work.
While on other days, hands join
in the creating of a unique masterpiece.

Stitch by stitch

An echo of laughter emanates from
a room where they gather.

Sometimes the mood is somber
There are also moments when tears
can no longer be held in check.

Designs evolve and come to life.
Pieces are shuffled while educated eyes
make bold or subtle choices and changes.
Size is determined
while conversation winds back and forth.

The color of thread involves
another long discussion
as do the upcoming fairs.
Events where these beauties
can be displayed and possibly sold.

Stitch by stitch

Quilts lovingly sewn
for family, for friends,
sewn for a multitude of good causes,
knowing in advance the meaning
of holding one in hand.

Knowing that some child, woman or man,
will curl up within its wondrous nurture
sighing in tranquil relief.

Knowing that while there,
present to the moment,
whether in the stitching,
the giving or the receiving,
the troubles of the world
for a short time
can be forgotten.

MOTHER'S DAY

This rain.
It's endless!

A day offering no sunshine,
no soft spring breezes,
no comfort.

Weather forecasts suggest
the night will offer neither moon nor starlight,
just more of this incessant downpour.
The skies are crying.

Words, words, words…
An exhausted and fragmented soul
can scarcely comprehend them.
Last words, nauseatingly cruel
and unexpected.

It's over. I'm leaving.
There are no more words necessary,
and none that would be adequate.

Eyes burn, tears are held back.
A shattered heart accompanies pimply sweat
while hands and legs tremor.
A profound sense of abandonment
is all that remains.

No familiar wave.
No sweet farewell.
No honk of the horn.

The compass is trained West.
This time, it is not simply for work.

No matter the effort
nothing can ever be as it once was.
The naïve dream is spent.

There's another person in this picture.
Competing would be useless.

The final choice has been made.
Tonight, that is more than enough truth.

Raindrops, tears, a muffled cry
against the wind intermingle.
While a shredded heart whispers
a final "Good bye."

There will never be another,
"See you soon."

FRIENDS OF BILL

Physical distance
Emotional deserts
Dissociated states
Narcissism
Uncontrollable rage

Medicated living
Suspicions and judgements
Aggression
Obsessive self-doubt
Self-harm

Carving the deepest of valleys
Desolate
Riding this road's cold shoulder

Isolated
Suicidal
Till revelation dawns

I am so alone, so broken
I am desperate for a hand to hold
Desperate for that special someone,
a mentor who for a change
will understand.

Craving something foreign.
A place within where
normal, conventional, predictable,
are *not* just words.

What is normal?
Do you know?
Can you please give me an answer?

Let me risk
Let me find strength
Let me move forward
Let me…

I'll find it hard to, "*Keep it Simple.*"
Yet my friend Bill, quiet and calm

has repeatedly said and written,
"For me, it's been the only way."

So today
I will let go
I will trust
I will surrender

Even if, fear crawls up my back
Even if, it feels life-threatening
Even if, all must change

Even if…

TAKING FLIGHT

Go little bird
try out your injured wing.
The Spirit's breath will keep you safe.

But should you weary or be afraid,
come back to me and rest awhile.
My palm will always await you
in case of need.

Go
take on the world

   …re-discovering that you can fly!

AS THE YEARS GO BY

Sleep well, my little beloved.
You, who have not the anxieties
and fears that entertain my mind,
nothing yet to abruptly awaken you
from your sleeping hours.

Rest grandchild, while the winds are calm within your mind.
If granted the years, you too will confront old age
and its impending struggles.

For now, you are free of the worries taxing an old man.
The world has not engulfed you in its madness.
Your eyes are not yet weary with disappointments.
You do not know what it is to have tried and lost.

Not like my fool dreams of a world in chaos and crisis:
headlines stamped indelibly on the surface of memory.
A world filled at times with visions
of narcissistic debauchery,
psychopaths, useless war and terrorism.

Life is deceivingly short.
Far too soon, you too will experience
the deepest of sorrows.
Loved ones you have treasured,
suddenly gone from this impermanent world.

When you are time-worn as I
leaning against an old wooden pew,

memory may be a challenge.
Recall of those precious years of childhood freedom
might become vaguer as the years go by.

Laugh, little one,
as Poppa and Momma share with you
rough and tumble play.

Remind me too, that being silly and giddy
while playing trivial games and make-believe
profits the soul.

Learn well, my precious beauty
as they teach you verses and song.
As you mature, you will recognize
that the gift of knowledge is fundamental
to wisdom and right choices.

Believe, my little one
that my love for you has no conceivable end.
You who endow me with countless moments
to cherish and share.

Give thanks, my little treasure.
As you grow you will better understand
the meaning of generosity and giftedness.

Pray for me, your Grand-Papa
who can at times be melancholy
and a bit miserable while confronting
the consequences of advancing years.

Peace be with you, as you lay your head
on soft and supple eiderdown till morning dawns.
I am filled with an immense gratitude

that you and I have been present to one another
on this quiet, sun-dappled day.

Grateful too, that I am still able to bend
and give you a wee kiss
as I wish you profound blessings
and the sweetest dreams this night can bring.

YOU ASK, "WHO ARE YOU?"

A bit of today, but a lot of tomorrow.
A few tears, yet a lot of laughter.
A few steps backward, but thousands forward.
A few failures, yet a lot of success.

Most of all, sharing everything
that needs to be shared.
Even in silence.

To me, *You* are joy.

SPIRIT

Does rain fall and drip
from frizzy hair?

Can snowflakes be captured
on a pink and extended tongue?

Do tears taste salty?
Who hears one's laughter?

Who hears one's cry,
when all is left is spirit?

FLY

Sinking, drowning
in welcome abandonment.
Leaning into wind and cotton candy clouds.
Crossing a threshold into the unfamiliar.

Suspended between ocean,
foothills and mountains.

The descent sublime,
gliding into the beauty
of desert lands and azure waters.

Later, a beach walk.
Head and heart swathed warmly
enveloped by a soft breeze,
surf and sound.

Glorious shades of sand swirl.
Countless cacti dot the dessert.
Such variety among the birdcalls,

chirping, "Hello!"
Wondrous colours shimmer.

Mister Rooster loudly declares the break of day.
Church bells herald dawn and noon.
Pack dogs announce sudden nightfall.
Starry moonlight proclaims
the final call of day.

Beauty; infinite.
Human appreciation and understanding;
finite.
Leading to new, boundless and precious encounters
planted upon the human heart.

Inviting humanity into glorious anthems
of gratitude and petition,
at times referred to as *hymn and prayer*.

Held within the spirit
an ethereal essence is then released,
lancing love words toward the heavens.

In the soft tranquil of daybreak
a benevolent invitation is heard.

"Today be…
　　　　　…Just Be."

RETREAT

The wind howls while I watch countless snowflakes
arrogantly showing off in a swirling, manic dance.

Ensconced and safe I curl up by the fireplace
at the foot of a mountain here at White Spruce.

Without rushing
Without planning
Without anxiety
Dwelling in the moment.

Watching
Waiting
For winter's storm to pass.

I feel, I think,
I write, I rest,
with no need to be elsewhere.

What a gift it is to remove oneself,
from the busyness of life!

EIGHTY

Eighty pods valiantly, yet reluctantly cling
to the branches of my weeping birch.
They are all that is left from this season's growth.
Soon they will scatter and disperse
in late-autumn's gusty wind.

I counted eighty twinkling lights
silvering my Marian grotto.
I was glad for their vivid warmth
on this damp and gloomy day.

I spread eighty lake pebbles before me
thinking of how singularly precious they appear.
Not one of them identical, just like humanity.

I watched eighty starlings bird-dancing.
Obliterating the dreariness of today's wintry sky.

I walked eighty steps.
I was grateful that I could.

I recited my night prayers,
noting that I have
repeated those calming words
many hundreds of times x eighty.

I wondered if my years would pass quickly.
Surprising me, as they did you.

Eighty times whatever number
will never serve
to count all the memories.
Nor the sudden moments of sadness
since you have been gone.

Eighty isn't much.
But when looked at
through the eyes of eternity,
it is enough.

TRAVELLING ON THE
WINGS OF THE WIND

Through the gift of imagination,
I soar.

Flying high
above this wondrous planet
I see the incredible gifts of water and land.

I see the length of journey it takes
to circumnavigate this phenomenon;
this living sphere.

I sigh,
eager for the contact of air against skin
while fluttering through wild oats
and avoiding sword-like grass.
Absorbing the sultry air
of more deserted places
and deep tropical forests.

Ice crystals shatter upon my cheeks.
Flying into the white-out of the bitter Arctic
the memory of a bonfire sustains me.

I feel the nurturing power of rain.
The frightening capacity
of tumultuous trade winds engulf me.

Prerequisites
if I am to behold four seasons,
each with its own beauty.

In the semidarkness of night
a moon reveals itself.
It plays games with differing shapes.
On differing continents
a crescent reversed
depending on where I fly,
shredding the only memory of the moon I know.

This is my world.
This is my point of origin.
This is my place in the cosmos.

This is my home,
for which I am eternally grateful.

DOES IT MATTER?

I get caught up in the hyperbole.
A worry-worm winds its way
through my veins.

I'm suffocating in its pressure
as it pushes me to perform more,
more and more!

"NOW. RIGHT NOW!"

Because in this world
action is achievement.
Work and constant busyness
equals accomplishment.

Will head and heart choose
the wonder and glory
of this precious stretch of time,
the exquisite tempo of lethargy,
without anxiety or guilt?

To wallow, as a soft breeze
makes an offering of a sweet caress,
inviting dust particles
to dance to its rhythm.

There is no harm in choosing to forego
laborious or even simple,
uncomplicated tasks.
In allowing time to rest, to do little,
to do less, to do nothing.

Nothing done or not done today
is likely to have permanent,
adverse consequences
nor lasting angst,
unless the old, deep-rooted voices win.

Coffee klatches or shopping time,
reading time or grandchild time,
auntie time, adult time, play time,
meditation and writing time…
none of it will be sincere
or a genuine act of giving
if the heart is longing to be elsewhere.

Friends, if they are such will understand.
Not judging but rather acknowledging
every body's need for occasional,
if not habitual silence and solitude.

The time has come for quieting the soul.
Time to trust and surrender.
Time to cherish what is within,
to listen and respond tenderly
to the directive of body and mind.

This is peace.
This is harmony.

And on this day
it is all that truly matters.

WORD GAME

PRAY~ for someone will hear.
GIVE~ for someone will receive.
FEEL~ and let it seep into your being.

SEEK~ it is the route to profound answers.
OFFER~ because you have such abundance.
LISTEN~ it will lead to wisdom.

PRAISE~ because you, are You.
GRANT~ favors, without expectations.
FORGIVE~ and your heart and soul will smile.

TALK~ even in fear of making a mistake.
TREAT~ with respect and kindness, all of creation.
APPRECIATE~ the give and take in all relationships.

Most importantly,
LOVE~ yourself.
For you are worthy!

STONE COLD

A sense of desolation descends.
An intense, cloying feeling
never experienced.

All that is left is a cold isolation
squeezing a damaged heart
making breath ragged.

When distanced and wounded like this
there is a deep desire, a profound hunger
to climb onto a high stone shelf,
to hide from the curious looks
and interfering questions.

Closing eyes against a world
that has caused hurt and doubt.
Well, not the world really...

This consuming distress
of adolescent heartbreak
was never anticipated.

Innocence can no longer protect
from the pain, the misery
of this permanent good-bye.

The daydreams once dreamt have perished.
Along with the flame of yearning
and the hope of *forever*.

Dreams of an eternity together.
Words that said, ever-more.
That no one and nothing
could ever hinder love.

Was it all a big mistake?
A misinterpretation?
An unintentional error in judgement?

Something that should never have
evolved into commitment.
Into oaths whispered in the dark.

Crying over broken promises
bravery has vanished.
With not a clue as to what comes next.

Something sacred and beautiful is gone.
And all there is left, are small gifts to hold.

CELEBRATING 2017 ~ CANADA's 150ᵗʰ

Smiling faces and many graces
within the seen and unseen
of a community of the heart.

Generations taking care of one another.
Our elder's stories; sacred,
honoured with love and gratitude.

Parents who sacrifice to provide
this "small town" atmosphere
and multi-recreational environment.
Opting for a safe and wondrous place
for themselves, their children
and their neighbours.

A marvellous melding of various arts,
culture, sports, business and tourism.
Tucked among holistic healers, potters,
woodworkers, builders, musicians, poets,
living the everyday drama of life.

A deep-seated, innate feeling
that one need never to be alone, or lonely
unless seeking repose and solitude.

A shared understanding
of what unity means.

Whether through joy or sorrow,
life or death, success or crisis,
all is recorded upon the heart
and treasured.

It is the affirmation received
while dwelling upon nature's gifts.
The rising and setting of the sun,
embraced by the mountain's
staggering peaks and shadowed valleys.

The change of seasons:
their unique and exceptional gifts.

A deep knowing that we can all,
'Bloom, where we are planted.'

It's the story of most small towns
but especially true of mine.

REMEMBER

On this day the dawn hours declare
a new year for you.
Do with it what you most desire.

Whatever you choose, remember:
Life is a quick breath
caught up by the wind.
At times, too soon gone.

That laughter and tears go hand in hand.
Without knowing both intimately,
you will miss much.

That a day without hope
is a day lost to the soul.

That faith will carry you through
the most poignant of joys
and the inevitable sorrow.

If you remember and trust in all these things
you will soon realize and appreciate
that without love, laughter,
tears and hope,
this right of passage
would not be so amazingly precious.

SAYING GOOD-BYE

Tacky sap drools down a lodgepole pine.
Making satisfied sounds
the nuthatch hides her seeds protectively.

The pileated woodpecker has become
King of the Forest these last days.
Rat-tat-tatting he begs for a fall reprieve
from the frigid weather to come.

Having scattered the last of the seed-stock,
chipmunks race by with bulging cheeks.
Yet, still able to sound out a 'Thank-you!'

The *Kook* is slowly receding toward its source.
Next spring, this river will swell and become a lake
providing us with a miles-long reservoir.
Affording us indescribable hours of entertainment.

The labor of early morning or late afternoon fishing
is often blessed with a catch of freshwater salmon
to be griddled on a flagrant fire,

or smoked and preserved
for a sweet and crisp winter treat.

The boats are few now.
Nature's sounds are lively,
more pronounced.

Camps are looking more and more barren,
as they are returned to their undisturbed
and natural state.

All trace of human presence and habitation gone,
till next spring blooms, when once again
the many sites are re-established,
leading to numerous, eventful,
recreational opportunities.

This new, bitter season
will provide less sustenance
to birds, squirrels, local bovine and deer.

Bracing for the cold,
it will require more effort,
as the snow flies and the wind bites.

The equinox moon,
informing us of summer's end
will soon show its pumpkin-colored face.
Blurring, obscuring, the billions of stars
we are so privileged to enjoy in this blackened darkness.

There are memories recorded, trees planted.
Barges and a variety of watercraft
are pulled onto trailers and readied for storage.
Boats are winterized and tarped,
motor oils put away.

Larch trees ready for the wintry burial of fallen needles.
The only coniferous here to shed this season's coat.

The time has come to put away summer
and encounter winter,
with its own abundance of enriching gifts.

Such is the glory of this annual, regimented ritual,
manifesting both joy and quiet sorrow.

One gladly repeated from season to season.

DARK NIGHT

Is such profound emptiness a curse?

The feeling is not dissimilar
to a package of rattling contents,
broken and of little use.

There are sorrows that tonight,
are excruciating,
a pain that is hardly bearable.

Sobs are the singular sound
in this room.

Tonight, caught in this hopeless
passage through time
there is no revelation, no answer.

How does one empty the mind
of this constant, tedious voice?

Spewing ugly, damning words,
one heaped upon the other.

Brought upon by desperation,
blistering heartbreak and shattered dreams.

This night wreaks of relentless pessimism.

Body and soul
strapped down by invisible cords.

Powerlessness deadening
the existence of joy.
The capacity to delight
in the wondrous movements of life.

Where is the other voice?
The lost voice, acknowledging worth
and a sense of wholeness?

Where is the glue to repair
these countless, fragmented bits,
cementing them into one?

In this universe of lakes, rivers, oceans
and streams, of sand, land and trees,
where is *self* found?

It is time for the closing of eyes
on this difficult, trying day,
praying that dawn will bring relief.

For somewhere within
there is faith in tomorrow.

A small microscopic grain of confidence
trusting that a new day will bring hope.
That sacred blessings will bring answers.

That scrap, that granule of confidence
permitting a resolute belief
that insanity cannot
and will not,
devour this soul.

CREATION EXCLAIMS

In the blush of the peach-mango coloring
of the sunrise.

In the heart of rolling hills
abruptly steeping into the cerulean sky.
Bald peaks exposed in praise.

In clouds, greys stacked one upon the other,
overwhelming morning's early, yellow clarity.

In the still waters of an autumn lake
whose lazy current meanders south
changing benignly from vast expanse
to narrow river.

In the breath of the soft wind
caressing my cheek
I sit and ponder its touch at water's edge.

Aware of the vibrancy of duck, loon,
coot, osprey, heron and eagle.

They, who also mourn summer's end
with woeful evening calls
while darkness settles in weary bones.

In the smoke that rises from campfires
warming night's cold shoulder
soothing body and spirit alike.

In night's starry glow, backlit by a soft
orange-faced moon,
gently providing secours
to night creatures below.

Such wonder and awe
as Creation exclaims its spectacle
of *Universal Love*.

RECOLLECTIONS of SIMONE
~ A short story ~

Mountain ferns sway in a stiff breeze.
Strong and resilient, just as she was.
As I gather colorful lake stones
I recollect her passion for life,
nature and learning.

Rocks arrayed throughout the yard's
impressive flower gardens and in her
turn-of-the-century, Victorian home.
They were also permanent fixtures
among books and house plants.
The memorabilia of a lifetime.

Tulips are bursting with bloom here,
a multitude of riotous color
reminding me of the terry-cloth beach robe
she immaculately stitched,
marrying two large beach towels.

Forty years later it is mine to wear
as I walk the rocky shore of Lake Koocanusa.
Proud owner of this psychedelic relic
zipper still intact, pockets at the ready
for more lake treasures.

Pussy willows, Wild Rose reds, Saskatoon blossoms,
Lilac's purple bunches, Irises' mottled yellows,
are all reminders of her artistic genius.

Anything white, fluffy and feathery,
is reminiscent of the marabou lovingly tacked
onto the collar of a floor length gown of red velvet.

Her own pattern designed and edited
while her imagination blossomed.
Meticulously sewn
on a New Year's Eve afternoon.
Preparation for a last-minute date-decision
with the man of her life.

Nails freshly painted, her coiffure a "French roll,"
decorated with a luminescent, white pearl hair comb.

His black brogues polished to a gleam,
tied with new rolled laces that had been tucked away,
at the ready, for just such a grand occasion.

They left to dine and dance the night away.
Radiant faces glowed, as they no doubt owned the floor
with their mastery of steps and rhythm.

I look at the shoe selection for this season
and wonder, "Is she wearing wedges, kitten heels,
or stilettos, as she peacefully wanders
through her heavenly paradise?"
I'd bet on the stilettos!

A friend who takes pity on my lack of baking skills
delivers an occasional fresh loaf of white bread
that looks and smells just like Maman Simone's!

Occasionally, the gesture brings a tremor to my throat
and a tear to my eye.
I feel again the sudden loss of two mothers.
Their demise separated by mere weeks.
These were women who seemed to instinctively know
their way around a stove and oven!

I see brand new Nissan cars on the road.
The sight of them brings out a giggle.
I'm wondering if she's the angel
defending the wheel this time round?
Keeping a highway driver safe at 130 kliks
in a 100-kilometer zone,
as she had been prone to doing!

I revel in the connection to each of my senses.
Particularly the seasonal sounds and smells
of baking, canning and pickling.

Lazing back in an Adirondack chair
I close my eyes and recall
the zing of the wire cable,
as Maman and we older siblings took turns
pulling fresh laundry off the line.

Whites and fragile colors were dashed with water,
from an obsolete, deep bronze beer bottle
topped with a dented and ancient sprinkler:
origins unknown.

Linens stored in the freezer till ironing day,
usually a Saturday.
These days permanent press is invaluable
but there will always be cottons on my line
that need some additional care.

Pulling shirts, handkerchiefs, dresses
and pillowcases from their icy prison,
the smell of humectant hung in the air.

A hot iron descended upon ice cold fabrics
sounding out a satisfied sizzle,
as blistering hot iron met cloth.

The unraveling of a new bolt of polyester material
rustled with static.
An ear tuned to the crinkly resonance of a McCall's
or Simplicity pattern, being gently opened
as to not tear the fragile contents.

More memories reveal themselves.
The click-clack of high heels on century old maple floors.
The smell of Pledge, a favorite wood polish,
the lingering odors of Johnson's floor wax,
paint, wallpaper glue, shellac and veneer.

Barbeques, the glowing embers of a campfire,
swimming at dusk, and star filled evenings
accented by a ritualistic cup of Red Rose tea.

Croquet, games of Hide and Seek
or maybe Charades,
while chewing a rare treat of Chiclets
or the soapy taste of "Thrills" gum,
with evenings culminating in
the requisite toasted marshmallows.

All these memories bring back
those indelible tastes, sounds and scents,
of life on the prairie.

Summer also brought on the hunt
for lakes and campgrounds.
Those places where six youngsters
could literally, "run wild!"

It is good to recall the crackling spine
of a new book on its premiere opening.
Along with Maman's skill at the piano,
how she annually refreshed
her finger's memory
while diligently following the notes
of her youth's 1940's sheet music.

Nail polish: Corals and reds
Remover: Acetone
Hairspray: Stiff and almost certainly toxic.

Time brings back the cheers of ecstasy
over the New York Yankees pennant triumphs,
while gathered around
the fourteen-inch turquoise radio.

Thrilled to know every stat on our favorites:

Hank Aaron, Micky Mantle,
Yogi Berra, Willie Mays,
our home filling with raucous cheering.

Reveling in the action of the All-Star Games!
Remembering vividly the wins and losses.

The hiss of a Labatt's "Blue," opened at the start
of a Saturday Night Montreal Canadiens hockey game.

Jean Beliveau, Bernie Geoffrion, Gilles Tremblay,
Henri Richard, Maurice Richard, Guy Lafleur.
Our hockey heroes!

And the hiss sounded again
while we sat in guarded readiness.

Yearning... hungering... for the Home Team's win.
Forever faithful to the Canadian Football League's
Winnipeg Blue Bombers,
noting the disappointments of 1967:

4 wins/12 losses in our Centennial year!

Eventually, the tink of an empty
dropped into its cardboard case.

Always glass, usually a "24."
Ah… the long-held memories!

My thoughts slowly wander back to the present.
I sigh, looking upon the St. Francis sculpture I inherited.
A treasure planted into my lake garden,
just as it was in hers.

While I watch with amusement
birds chatter incessantly,
the nose-diving battle is on.

Who will be first at the birdbath?
It is a very comic avian display,
one that warms my heart to watch.

Fatigued by the blazing sun, I close my eyes.
"Fear not," I hear a strong but soft voice whisper.
"Those whom you have lost are so very jubilant,
delighting in many an exotic garden.

They surround you and protect you,
looking forward to the occasional chats,
and your prayerful incantations.
Be at peace."

And on this precious day…
                                    …I am.

ILLUMINATION

It is time to open wide
the hearts of our communal humanity
that all eyes might see the realities of hate
and the faces of love.

It is time to put value to truth
and counter falsehood, at all costs.
Time to be a people of compassion
not confrontation.

Let us open wide our gift of speech
that every word be a loving action,
that we may touch the wounded
in their pain.

May we encourage one another
to walk a path of justice and humility,
opening wide our abilities to serve
rather than being self-serving.

Open wide the skies this night,
and invite glorious peace
to rain *Light and Truth*
upon our world.

MY GRANDS ~ A DAISY, A ROSE, AND TWO LITTLE MEN

My precious gift.
Resolute in calling them
my absolute favorites!

They are teaching me to be more patient
to be more forgiving
to not be afraid to show real emotion.

They teach me a different kind of faith:
faith, even when things are stressful
and particularly complicated.

They show that I can move on.
We can shake-off whatever is troubling
with confident conviction.
Believing that genuine hope and change
truly exist.

They are teaching me
more compassion toward others.
That bench buddies can really make
an intentional difference
in the life of a classmate.

They are teaching me to be a better listener.
Though, I do fail at that
more often than I should.
Yet, they allow me my defects.

They remind me that occasionally
a time-out is necessary to one's sanity.

They make it evident that to walk away,
is also at times the better choice.
They *get* that from time to time
I may be 'in one of those moods.'
That I too may be in need
of a generous, simple hug.

They know it is acceptable to get impatient
with Mimi's sermons.
And they are not afraid to tell me so.

They teach me there is always time
for puddle dances and catching raindrops
or snowflakes on the tip of the tongue.
That it is perfectly ok to draw outside the lines.
On purpose or not!

They allow me to waken to the wonder of imagination,
the true pleasure dress-up and dance parties can be.

They are sometimes sad.
Loss is part of their vocabulary.
Two of them know what it is to grieve
especially for their Nana.

In their wondrous innocence
they spontaneously agree
she is now in the happy place
our family calls heaven.

I can also reassure them with calming words
when they pose profound questions.

So that when the time comes
they'll know the way home

and be encircled
by Nana's hugs once more.

Simultaneously, they are a million things
and one small thing, of which I am a part.

Nothing they do is trivial or insignificant.
Each one is a unique, inspiring little being.

They are my beloved.
I will cherish them,
forever
and a day.

QUESTIONS

Should you have the privilege to ask one last question,
what would it be?
Would it be, "Why me?"

Or would you sigh and whisper,
"I am ready. I am moving on."

Should you recall one aspect of your life
would it evoke memories
of all you did not try… or do?
Or would you reminisce about all
that you have accomplished?

If you had one thing left to do,
would it be action
or would it be prayer?

If you could speak one last phrase
would it be, "I only wish…"
or would you softly say,
"I have fully loved!"

Would there be memories of joy
or would there be too many regrets?

No moment is promised but the present.
Live it.
Live it to the fullest.

For on this day…
                    …you have a choice.

SOME

Some would call it a waste of time
simply sitting in an Adirondack chair,
feet resting upon a leather footstool
crafted eons ago.

Some would wonder
what worth these moments have.

Listening to the chatter of a red squirrel
saying, 'Hello.'
Punctually joined by the spotted ground squirrel
with an orange belly, whistling 'Goodnight,'
while welcoming her babies home.

Some might worry the old boat
would spring a leak while out on the *Kook*.
Therefore saying, 'No thanks!'
to an exciting exploit.

Some folks feel safe
tucked into a tent or trailer,
not anxious about nocturnal visits
from little critters in whose territory we reside.

Some cannot see the beauty and adventure
of living raw
choosing to live without electricity,
running water or cable television.

Some may not appreciate
the endearing camping community
who often call themselves 'family.'
Established by common activity and goals
where friendship blooms.

Some are willing to risk
the sound of loud generators,
dirt bikes, quads and jet boats.

Or the occasional echo of music
thundering through stereo systems
that would likely suffice in a stadium.

Some prefer the evening sounds
of the forest for company,
reverently shared with camping comrades.

And most are willing to accept
the occasional imposition

when a request for help
can hinder leisure time.

Many have said, "Yes,"
to things that may not be perfect,
as perfection is not the goal.

Seeking only to be one with land and lake,
with the open roads and seamless boundaries.
Giving honor to this earthly paradise.

FARE WELL

Walk child, through the veil
of heaven's gate
while angels call your name.

Eternal life and love
is the promise given to all
who lean on the
assuring power of faith.

You, my child,
believed heaven's promise
from the depths of your heart.

Your time has come to watch over us.
You are a shining star in our night sky.

No more angst.
The fears forever gone.

Cherished.
Now held in perpetual love.

Sing my child
as you dance through paradise.
Sing among the angels you loved so well.

ALLELUIAH

Eagle circling, river rushing.
The last of the ice blocks
ride the current.
Azure sky, quiet breeze.

The first days of spring have arrived.
It is easy to marvel at the world's
brilliant display of colors,
while standing before this majestic landscape.

Meanwhile, the heart questions,
pondering what surprises summer might bring.
Will there be fulfilment of the dreams dreamt
and visions seen?

Will grace, blessing and opportunities
showered upon this season be acknowledged?

Will innumerable choices
bring solutions to what is sought?
Ones that reflect the best of who we are?

Many of life's most pressing questions are posed
with few profound answers.

Questions take time to be formed,
and often, lapses of time to be answered.

By choice, there are always sufficient hours
and days to heed the deep-felt voice of *Spirit*.
A soul voice.
A providential voice,
knowing every need and every solution.

Answers disclosed
according to a much greater authority.

Not according to the impatient desire,
to instantly hold answers
in the palm of the hand.

MOVING ON

Peddle my friend,
up that lofty mountain trail
straining to reach the other side.

Peddle with head held high.
Dignity will direct your course.

Peddle, shuffle, peddle, shuffle,
toward your ultimate destination.

Riddled with pain
your skin is a sheen of sweat.

A never-ending anguish
batters at your broken body.

Forget the angst
of things unsaid.
Undone.

Quiet your anxious spirit,
that fading life-force within you.

Let it be.
Let it all be
enough.

Do not fear,
for love awaits.

Perfect Love
for a perfect eternity.

NATURE'S GIFT

Here I am at the bottom of the wind's gust.
All things that surround me
thrown about by fierce air.

I crouch in a small indentation among the cliffs,
a pocket protects me,
assuring shelter among the willows, wild roses,

poplars, lilacs and long grasses that blow
along the edges of the babbling creek.

No need to fear.

No need to move from this tiny cocoon
where the gusting gale
has become wholly silent.
A little enclave of peace.

I am safe.

SUMMER'S END

Feather upon feather
the eagle braces its wings
against a rushing wind.

Tips beat forcefully
anticipating the movement
of bitter autumn air.

Regal magnificence
sweeping gracefully
below mottled cloud.

With clenched jaw and gripping talon
he dives fearlessly,
swooping, stalling,
swift and sure
shattering the mirrored glass.

Circle upon circle
green-gold ripples ensue,
startling the fish abruptly clutched
from its fluid environment.

Clenched jaw, gripping talon,
wrestle for domination.

Succumbing,
this water creature has seen
its earthly end.

No mercy granted.
None expected.

White head, shimmering tail,
sparkle brilliantly against
a solitary ray of sun.

Angling north,
he rides the current
of the south-east breeze.

Heading home
to share a succulent feast
of meat and bone.
To rest high above this floor
of coniferous wonder.

Sated
Glorious
Majestic
Free

I revel in its presence,
grateful for the gift of sight.

And the seeming protection,
an omen of good fortune.

A blessing…

        …as summer comes to pass.

FRIENDS

Friendships are like stones
gathered at water's edge.

Each unique.
Each with their own composition.

Pattern
Shape
Color
History

Friendships are like rippling water.
Waves upon waves of nurture.

Sharing
Caring
Crying
Laughing

Friendships are like clouds
hovering to give shade
when the sun is too bright.
Or rain, when life needs watering.

Friends…
Needed
Cherished
Welcomed

A safe, beloved harbor.

CELEBRATE

Ocean beats upon the shore.
Palm trees sway prayerfully.

Sand art displays flourish
created by hurling, heaving waves.

Tree branches shine brightly
adorned with colored
columns of light.

Gatherings abound.
Cheer is shared.

Bells are ringing.
Choral voices resound.
Presents wrapped
while candles dance.

A star.
A stable.
A straw creche and figurines assembled
below the fronds of a small palm.

Proclaiming the wonders of this December day.
Given to all who long to receive.

TREASURE

The chest is deep.
Filled with gold, silver,
diamonds, opals and rubies.

It has laid sunken
in ocean depths,
waiting to be released
from the sands of time.

Waiting to become valued
for its true worth.

Waiting to surface
and be exposed.
Shining brightly
in the light of day.

The treasure is great.
The treasure is *You*.

"S" WORDS

Surrender to all aspects of love.
Surround yourself with light and all its gifts.
Search for what is good and right.

Scatter compliments.
Silence wrong voices with truth.
Seek that which brings you genuine peace.

Serve where and when you can.
Submit to the moment.
Savor your life's true passion.

Knowing that you never walk alone.

CHÈRE MAMAN

Poetic words are not adequate
to tell you how much I love you.

How as I age, I understand you more.
Accept you, just as you were given to me.
I intended to tell you this more often
before you were taken from us.

Today, I wish to dwell
in the womanhood
you so bravely gave me.

My soul quietens,
absorbing into my spirit
all that creation has abundantly provided.

I am incredibly proud
to be your eternal child.
The first you bore.

Your first experience of birth
and motherhood.

Thank-you for all that was
and all that is yet to be
in my blessed life.

FAREWELL TO WINTER'S PARADISE

You will find no Kentucky bluegrass here.
Saint Augustine's blades creep
along the silty, sandy ground.

So robust and resilient is this grass
that extreme heat slows
but does not diminish its progress
as it connects one sprout to another.
Oblivious to other vegetation's
intrusive growth.

The more somber sage color
of a few straggling weeds
mixes with the deepest green

of flourishing clover patches.
All intertwined in this desert vista
while greying tempest clouds roil above.

This burgeoning grass garden
is edged with a number of desert plants.

The most beautiful
the multi-petaled yellow hibiscus.

A younger deep coral, single-petaled neighbor
battles unsuccessfully to claim the most blooms.
It is a yearlong race
through tumultuous wind, rain, heat and drought.

Ficus, bougainvillea and cacti stand sentinel
around this portion of concrete terrace,
a surface that is a delightfully
welcoming chill to scorched bare feet.

Robust sunshine will help birth
mixtures of luscious blossoms
such as the magnificent Desert Rose.

Roots of potted plants at times
escape their confines
wrapping in circles at the base of clay,
ceramic, and other varying vessels.
Nature's artistry so wondrously bestowed
upon humankind.

Succulents, such as aloe
and an array of yucca species
tolerate cooler winter climes
as well as the sweltering,
suffocating, dog days of summer.

Extremes that end in torrential rains
are at times accompanied
by the vicious hurricanes of early autumn.

Blinking and dancing strings
of solar-powered lights
offer warmth to evening's call.

Hummingbirds approach feeders
for their last pull of nectar.
Majestically dressed, they flit about
playing one last game of tag,
as do the juvenile iguanas
living next door on a naked, rugged lot.

Infant sparrows tug worms and ants
from the freshly mowed grass.

A slight breeze teases the wind chimes
offering sublime notes to the darkening vista.

I sit in the dusky, shadowed evening,
awed by this newfound home
that allows me to flee from the inescapable
wintry cold of Western Canada.

As light fades,
I am reminded that this day
must end in sleep.

Saying goodnight to my surroundings, I smile.
Ready for more of tomorrow's morning miracles.

MY HOME IN YOU

Let me come into your house.
In you let me abide.
There are times I feel neglected
and crave a constant friend.
One who is welcoming,
sharing without fear.

Let me come into your house
where a muted light always shines
and a resting place awaits,
where we speak such tender words.

Let me come into your house
where the door is open wide.
Where shadows do not follow
and a feast of peace is laid.

Let me come into your house
that place within your soul
where a touch
can make a difference,
and my arms
crave to embrace.

Let me heal the place that hurts
and rid you of your pain.
Let me join with you in laughter
where no trace of shyness lies.

Then one day, I will welcome you
where your room I will provide.

A place of quiet gifting,
in the hands of love's refrain.

AWE-STRUCK

The absolute stillness of this dawn
will define the day.
Yet, an earth-shifting tremor
claimed and defined the night.

In the glory of the full moon
the planet danced,
as Mother Nature asserted her right
to move mountains.

The lazy undulating waves
of the lake had rolled gently
through evening's darkening light.

In sudden shock they rear,
reversing direction
with a certain violence
as a howling wind disrupts
the quiet air of earlier hours.

Coyotes, disturbed from their
restful sleep yelp loudly,
dashing out from their sandy dens.
Piercing night's silence
with their distressing sounds.

Terrified dogs frothing at the mouth,
panicked and petrified,
form packs and race aimlessly
unsure of where to seek safety,
during this devastating midnight hour.

I become a sentinel of the night,
in awe of this earthly realm's ability
to alarm and astonish.

Eventually, I say good-bye
to the waning moon
and my surroundings.

Ready to drift into a soothing,
dreamless sleep.

A brief smile of joy ~
my last conscious moment.
For it is rare to fall witness
to an occasion such as this.

And rare also, that it only caused
this mountainous terrain
to quake and tremble,
without a cataclysmic disaster.

And for that, we can all be
especially grateful.

ROOTS

Ribbons of life below the desert soil.
The soul of every tree, shrub and plant,
rooting and nosing as they feed
from the earth below.

Our own roots are undeniable.
They may be deep or shallow,
close or distant.

We all have a history.
Life's DNA, shared.

Every root affects our humanity
whether visible or intangible.
Personality traits, particular patterns
and behaviors pulse through each of us.

Tics, gestures, tones of voice
and innate characteristics
resound within those roots,
often handed down
from generation to generation.

There is no escaping.
Each of us is affected,
individually and collectively.

Yet rootedness,
that place from which we have come
should not define our options.

History ... is history.
Blame should not be levied.
Shame should not be carried.

The good
should be remembered
and celebrated.

Roots impact each living being
from conception to birth,
culminating in inevitable death.

Creative endeavor, broader knowledge,
wisdom and culture, can always be added
to roots of compassion, joy,
growth, forgiveness,
and faith.

The choice is ours to make.
Roots will become our personal
and common legacy.

Something that should likely not
be left up to chance!

THE CALL

Branches twist through broken trees.
The snap and crackle easily heard
from inside the chalet.
Plunging from great heights
they pile up on the frosty ground.

A mass of rolling leaves
creates autumn's Equinox dance.
Tumbling colors, one upon the other.

Geese are pulled along
by a breath-ripping wind,
circling through ice crystals
that are not quite snowflakes.
Descending to the wetlands below
they will find reprieve from the weather.

Nature, reminding the world once more
of its forceful impact
constant in showing its many
intriguing and beguiling faces.

The gusting and blowing is not gentle today.

Pushing aggressively, claiming, nudging,
in a not-so-quiet way.

Reminding all to listen, to hear,
to interpret the *Spirit Wind* within.

There is a choice,
a decision to be made here,
to ignore or acknowledge
its bold and fearless presence.

GENESIS ~ A Meditation.

Quieting my being
I sink into a vigilant solitude.

The surrounding chirp of birds
becomes nearly inaudible
as does the nattering of squirrels.

I no longer hear the hiss of rocks
in the ebb and flow at the water's edge.

The sound of soft pattering rain
indulges this time of restfulness.

Beyond the clouds the sun hums,
waiting patiently
for its own time to shine.

I bring my deepest consciousness
to the beating of my heart.
Its energetic pulse pushes life's fluid
through highways of veins and arteries.

I sense points opening and closing.
Letting redness and blueness
feed my humanity.

I begin to feel the buzz of a constant current.
I am mesmerized by this fascinating charge,
firing neurons
allowing me the power to be.

Without any conscious request
this flux of energy gives me life.

A twitch reminds me of the large muscle

answering cerebral requests in milli-seconds.
A mass so profoundly exquisite
as to be beyond even a limitless,
human imagination.

Reacting to directives from this extremely
complex grey matter, nerves tweak,
searching out the precise pathways needed
to accomplish their tasks.

While pondering, I rise
swaying back and forth to the music
playing its notes within me.

I am held upright by an astounding array
of bits and parts.
Aspects that could not sustain life
if not supported by a spectacular structure of bone.

Building blocks upon which all else is securely fastened.
Ensconced in a generous package called skin
that encompasses the whole of me.

I stretch and breathe deeply.
Two sacs of delicate tissue
accept and purify the outside air,
making it perfect in this continual nourishing
of the manifestation that is ~ me.

I have come to a slow realization
during this time of contemplation.

I am somewhat amazed to discover
a new appreciation, a new insight.
A deep and profound conviction
has soundlessly surfaced.

An inner voice murmurs a potent truth.
My physical construct is sacred, whole,
unique, wondrous, and safe.

Tranquil and at peace...
　　　　　　...when I choose to make it so.

DISCOVERING

Will I find you in the crackling of the fire
or in the glow of its quiet embers?

Will I feel you in the intense heat of a summer sun
or in the cooler rays of an evening sunset?

Will I find you in the fury of a storm–tossed sea
or in the diamonds cast upon its calmness?

Will I sense you in the empty darkness
or in the wash of pale moonlight
spread over my world?

Will I exalt you upon a mountain peak
or in the serene welcoming of the forest floor?

Will I find you in the wicked winter storm
or in the patterns of frost
that dance across my windows?

Will I sense you in the texture of the lives around me
or will I drink of the fruits of life
in the solitude of silence?

I bow before the majesty of my surroundings
and feel, and find, and know your presence
in the very essence of all creation.

And in this moment, I surrender myself
to the *Living Spirit.*

Within my trembling heart,
I surrender to everlasting love,
shown to me in all that
Perfect Love
has wrought into being.

~ *DEDICATIONS* ~

I would like to thank my sisters Nicole, Rita and Alice who have supported me through thick and thin. Your time given to this project is immeasurable. Without you, this work would not be what it is. Merci!

JAZZ: *LKMC*

ROCK CANDY: Nicole B. & Grand-mère extraordinaire.

FIRE: In honor of every fire fighter, every emergency responder within North America, who do all to protect us, while often endangering their own precious lives.

IS THIS LIVING?: Roger M.

SURRENDER: Uncle Gary and Auntie Jan ~ May she Rest in Peace.

YOU ~ MY STRENGTH: Victoria L.

DEAREST CHILD: Janine K.

WITNESSING TO LOVE: *WATBC* ~ our Bubbie

THE DREAM: Franzeska Rose F.

SEW WELL: To the Quilters Guild of Fernie BC., Canada

RETREAT: Thank-you *KDF*.

CELEBRATING 2017 ~ CANADA'S 150TH: The precious community of Fernie, BC., Canada

REMEMBER: *LSTC*: 2001

RECOLLECTIONS OF SIMONE: To my "*Forest*" siblings.

A ROSE, A DAISY AND TWO LITTLE MEN: Thank-you to such great parents. You know who you are!

TREASURE: Rachelle C.

~ *IN MEMORY OF* ~

IMPACT: Barry J.

THE SHARING OF QUERIES: In honor of all the players, families, those lost, those injured, and all who supported the Humboldt Bronco Hockey Team, and Organization of Humboldt, Saskatchewan, Canada after the tragic bus accident of April 16th, 2018, claiming the lives of sixteen of the twenty-nine passengers.

EARLY MAY MEMORIES: Rest in Peace Papa ~ Monsieur André Forest

SPIRIT: Grammie Frankie and Grampa Cec Coultry

FARE WELL: Cherish S.

MOVING ON: Ken W.

INDEX

ABOUT THE AUTHOR

"I do not see these writings as a memoir," says author, Huguette M. 'Mike' Forest-Coultry. "I prefer to call much of this collection, everyone's story."

"It encourages us to value the waterways and roads we have travelled, while embracing the wondrous journey yet to be lived."

"This is a story of our search for light, joy, enthusiasm and optimism. It also welcomes us to examine our relationship to the world and to one another."

Mike can be contacted at
journeyingthewaters@outlook.com
and welcomes responses
to her works.